CHOOSING YOUR CAREER

by Brian Harris, B.A., M. Ed.

A Self-Directed Guide to Help You Identify
Your Interests, Abilities and Values to Help You
Choose the Career That is Best for You

ISBN 978-1460930885

Every effort has been made to ensure that the information contained in this book is accurate. Neither the publisher nor the author is engaged in rendering professional advice or services to the individual reader. The ideas, strategies and suggestions contained in this book are not intended as a substitute for consulting with appropriate professionals. Neither the author nor the publisher shall be liable or responsible for any loss or damage allegedly arising from any information or suggestions in this book.

CGS COMMUNICATIONS, INC.

TABLE OF CONTENTS

**"All our dreams can come true,
if we have the courage
to pursue them."**

Walt Disney

INTRODUCTION

This book is designed to help you find the best career for yourself. Is this important for you? Absolutely! Your career can have a direct impact on how you feel about yourself? If your career is something you really enjoy doing, you will go to work each day with enthusiasm, and this feeling can spill over into the rest of your life as well. If you hate your job, you may begin to hate everything else too. A poor career choice can contribute to unhappiness. A good career choice can help you feel fulfilled and live a meaningful life.

Choosing a career is a difficult task for most people. How many people do you know who love their jobs? If most people were honest about their career, they would say that their job is something they have to do to pay their bills. As I work with people who have been in a career field for more than twenty years (and sometimes far less than this), I often hear people say that they wish they could do something different. Most of these same people admit that choosing a career when they were a young adult was often a quick decision, often based on little research and/or self-evaluation, that seemed okay at the time, but after a while they woke up each morning wishing they really didn't have to go to work.

When you discover the best career for you, you will look forward to what you do each day. Your job will leave you filling satisfied, rather than disillusioned. The fulfillment you feel in your job will have a positive affect on your life away from work as well.

Most people feel uncertain, at some point, about their future. People ask themselves: "How do I know I am

Would you be a happier person if you found your perfect career?

making the right choice?", "What if there are no jobs when I finish my education or training?", "There are so many choices, how do I know which one is best for me?", and so on.

Choosing a career is one of the most important decisions you will face in your life. Taking some time to plan and think about this decision can be one of the best things you ever do for yourself. Although your best career may be different than what other people choose, there are some research findings backed up by real life experiences, that contribute to what makes the perfect career. These findings could be summarized as follows:

1) Find a career that best matches your interests.

2) Find a career that best matches your abilities.

3) Find a career that best matches your values.

CHOOSING YOUR CAREER can help you in all three of these areas.

First, you will identify your interests. The questionnaire you will use to do this is based on material which I developed to help college students and adults to identify their interests. As I worked with thousands of adults and students, the number one concern expressed to me related to their career planning was often "Which careers best match my interests?" This chapter can help you to answer this question.

Secondly, you will explore your abilities. Your abilities need to support your interests in order for the career to be

What factors would contribute to a career being perfect for you?

the best one for you. There is no sense dreaming about being a professional baseball player if you can't throw or hit a baseball, and there is no sense dreaming about being a famous singer if you can't sing in tune or stand up in front of an audience. Your perfect career will combine both your interests and abilities in a harmonious manner.

Thirdly, you will identify your values and understand how your values affect both your happiness and satisfaction in a career. Understanding your values can help you realize what is most important to you. When all areas of your life honor your values, you will live a happier, more fulfilling life.

Create your own good luck through careful planning.

CHOOSING YOUR CAREER can assist you as you attempt to discover which career is the right one for you. For most people, there is not just one magical perfect job. For most people there are generally several jobs within a career field that best match your values, interests and abilities. Understanding the concept of related careers within career fields (which will be explained further in this book) can not only help you find the perfect job now, but at some point in the future if you find yourself unemployed (or underemployed), understanding this concept can help you to find the perfect job once again in your life.

Finding the perfect job can be a job in itself. It is recommended that you take your time and think carefully as you complete this book. Don't attempt to complete the material in this book in one evening. After each chapter, leave a day or two to think about what you have done. It is recommended that you share you results with a career counselor/advisor and others who know you well. In addition, share your results with a variety of people including those

One of the fastest ways to become successful is to find someone who is successful, and copy what they do.

who tend to support you in whatever you do, and also with people who tend to be more critical. Gather as much feedback as possible, and read other books related to this topic. One of the very best ways to discover the job that is best for you is to find people who really enjoy their careers. Take time to be with these people. Study them closely and learn from them. It has often been said that one of the fastest ways to become successful is to find someone who is successful, and then copy what they do.

Please note that I will use the words "career", "job", and "occupation" throughout this book as meaning the same thing.

CHOOSING YOUR CAREER is designed to help you discover the career that is best for you, it is not intended to actually help you get hired into this career. Another book in this series titled *GET HIRED* (additional information at the end of this book) can assist you in this process (such as writing resumes, answering interview questions, networking, etc.) by helping you to understand the six key factors employers are looking for when they hire.

As will be mentioned throughout this book, I recommend that you share your results in this book with a professional career counselor or advisor to help you better understand the careers that are most appropriate for you. The author of this book and publisher have neither liability nor responsibility to any person or other legal entity with respect to any sort of loss, or damage, or perceived damage caused, or alleged to have been caused by the information provided in this book. By reading this book, you fully accept these conditions.

SOME THOUGHTS ON CAREER SATSIFACTION

"To find a career to which you are adapted to by nature,
and then to work hard at it, is about as near to a formula
for success as the world provides."
Mark Sullivan

"A lot of people are afraid to say what they want
and that's why they don't get what they want."
Madonna

"A man cannot be comfortable without his own approval."
Mark Twain

"Look at a day when you are supremely satisfied at the end.
It's not a day that you lounge around doing nothing;
it's when you've had everything to do and you've done it."
Margaret Thatcher

"Nothing will work unless you do."
Maya Angelou

"Everyone chases after happiness,
not noticing that happiness is right at their heels."
Bertoit Brecht

"What does not satisfy when we find it,
was not the thing we were desiring."
C. S. Lewis

"Career success begins with career satisfaction."
Louise Garver

"If one advances confidently in the direction of his dreams,
and endeavors to live the life he has imagined,
he will meet with success unexpected in common hours."
Ralph Waldo Emerson

"Exert your talents and distinguish yourself."
Samuel Johnson

"Cheshire Puss," asked Alice, "Would
you tell me please which way
I ought to go from here?"
"That depends a good deal on where you
want to go," said the cat.
"I don't much care where," said Alice.
"Then it doesn't matter which
way you go, said the cat."
Charles "Lewis Carroll" Dodgsen

IDENTIFYING YOUR INTERESTS

Both success and happiness often result from being in a career where you enjoy what you are doing. In this first chapter, you will explore your interests and see how these relate to possible career choices. The career choices will help you to better understand how your interests relate to your career planning and also show you that there are likely several careers that best match your interests.

Like Alice, in the quote on page 10, if you don't know where you want to go, then it really doesn't matter where you head. Unfortunately, without direction you may bounce around from career to career without ever feeling a sense of satisfaction in what you are doing. Many people that I work with, who are unhappy in their careers, state that they never really gave much thought to the careers they selected. They often chose a career simply because it was readily available, or convenient, or was something their friends were doing, or something someone else told them they would be good at, and so on. Their lack of direction often resulted in working in jobs that were unfulfilling. They never took the time to discover their interests and then find careers that best matched these. Both success and happiness result from doing things that you enjoy doing.

Discovering what you enjoy doing requires some time for self-exploration. For some people, you may have lost track somewhere along life's journey of the things that really interest you. Each person has interests that are unique. The waitress in a restaurant may have an interest in working with customers that is quite different than the

Success comes from building on your strengths. Unfortunately, too many people have been taught to focus on their weaknesses, and as a result have a difficult time identifying their strengths.

When you move out of your comfort zone to learn more about yourself, you have the opportunity to achieve greater success and fulfillment in your career choice.

interests that a surgeon requires to be successful in the emergency operating room, but never-the-less, both of these people will encounter greater career satisfaction if what they are doing builds on their interests. Success comes from building on your strengths. Identifying your interests is one aspect of discovering your strengths. Another aspect of identifying your strengths is to identify your abilities which you will do in next chapter. When your interests and abilities support each other, you will discover your real strengths.

This chapter of *CHOOSING YOUR CAREER* focuses on exploring your interests. As you attempt to discover the best career for yourself, it is important to identify the things you have the strongest interest in. The remainder of this chapter provides questions (and scoring tables) to help you identify your interests. There are no right or wrong answers. The best answer is always what is best for you. Don't answer the questions by thinking about how others would want you to answer them. By listening to your own instincts, you will be able to identify your interests which in turn can be very useful to you in finding the perfect career for you.

As you work on pages 14 - 26, some questions may require some time and thought to answer, but your results will be worth this effort. For some people, these results will confirm what you are already thinking (which is a good thing) . For others, the results may open up a whole new world of possibilities (which is also a good thing).

Instructions are given on the following pages as to how to complete this next section of *CHOOSING YOUR CAREER*. The most important thing is that you are honest in answering the questions.

There are no time limits on completing these pages. Take as long as you want. If there are any words that you don't understand, it is okay to use a dictionary or to ask someone else for help.

As with any other part of this book, if you find yourself confused or frustrated by your results, it is strongly suggested that you consult with a career counselor/advisor to assist you in resolving any of your concerns.

Life has a lot to offer. Why shouldn't you enjoy it to the fullest?

On the next page you are going to be starting an interest survey. This will help you to identify your interests and some careers that best match your interests.

There are no right or wrong answers. Follow the instructions as they are given. In addition, there is no time limit. You can even ask others for help in understanding any words or instructions. Enjoy!

INSTRUCTIONS: In the following section, select the best statement for yourself from each group of five (you must select one answer each time) and print the number of your corresponding answer in the box beside the five statements.

From the following list, your best personal strength is . . .
1) your ability to write essays
2) your ability to organize
3) your ability to understand how to fix computer software problems
4) your ability in either music, drama, or art
5) your ability to resolve conflicts

You would make the greatest contribution to the building of a bridge if you . . .
6) helped to design the bridge
7) helped to present a workshop on the need for building the bridge
8) helped to estimate costs for the project
9) worked in actually constructing the bridge
10) provided first-aid support for any workers injured on the job

If you were applying for a job, you would likely apply for one . . .
11) where you were doing skilled work with your hands
12) where you were helping to promote a product
13) where you were meeting the leisure/recreational needs of others
14) where you could use your strong listening skills
15) where you were using your science related skills

From the following list, your best personal strength is . . .
16) your desire to help others
17) your reading skills
18) your keyboarding skills
19) your computer skills
20) your artistic skills

In ten years, you might best be able to write . . .
21) a book on how to provide excellent customer service
22) a book on evaluating the structure of buildings
23) a book on teaching children with learning disabilities
24) a book on accounting
25) a book on how to build a backyard shed

IDENTIFYING YOUR INTERESTS - PART A

INSTRUCTIONS: In the following section, select the best statement for yourself from each group of five (you must select one answer each time) and print the number of your corresponding answer in the box beside the five statements.

In ten years, you might best be able to write . . .
26) a book on medical research
27) a book on renovating houses
28) a book on marketing new products
29) a book on fitness
30) a book on effective selling techniques

In ten years which of the following do you feel you would best be able to write . . .
31) a book on some form of scientific research
32) a book related to family counseling
33) a book about cultural differences within our society
34) a book about office organization
35) a book about new advances in information technology

In which of the following situations would you be most helpful . . .
36) being part of a team developing an animated feature film
37) taking product orders by telephone or over the internet
38) helping to design a battery-powered car
39) helping to tutor kids who are struggling at school
40) assisting others with their investment planning

Your community is planning a special event. You could best help by . . .
41) setting up the stage and chairs
42) providing support for people with special needs
43) constructing a portable stage for the event
44) promoting the event
45) organizing either the food or recreational activities for the event

A job that would be most satisfying for you would involve . . .
46) some form of selling products and/or services to others
47) some form of applying your interest in science and mathematics
48) some form of counseling others
49) some form of applying your interest in geography and/or history
50) some form of clerical work or administrative assistance

INSTRUCTIONS: In the following section, select the best statement for yourself from each group of five (you must select one answer each time) and print the number of your corresponding answer in the box beside the five statements.

Your community is planning a special event. You could best help by . . .
51) helping to set up a website
52) helping to entertain the audience as a performer
53) helping to recruit volunteers
54) helping to design a portable stage
55) helping to organize and train the volunteers

If a company was developing a new product you could best help by . . .
56) helping to prepare a budget related to estimating costs
57) helping to package the product
58) helping to research any health issues related to the new product
59) helping to actually construct or manufacture the product
60) helping to create a television advertisement for the product

From the following list, your best strength is . . .
61) your ability to organize social events
62) your ability to understand the needs of others
63) your analytical skills in a science related discipline
64) your desire to help people who are encountering difficulties
65) studying great works of literature

Which of the following would you prefer to do . . .
66) prepare some letters to be sent to customers or clients
67) set up a wireless network for computers and printers in an office
68) create a company newsletter
69) assist customers who are returning damaged products
70) design a solar heating system for a new house

The greatest personal strength you would bring to a company is . . .
71) your ability to make effective presentations to others
72) your analytical mind in financial matters
73) your physical strength
74) your expertise in mathematics and science
75) your skills in repairing and/or operating machines

INSTRUCTIONS: In the following section, select the best statement for yourself from each group of five (you must select one answer each time) and print the number of your corresponding answer in the box beside the five statements.

Which of the following achievements would be most satisfying for you . . .
76) writing a book on advertising
77) writing a book to promote tourism in your country
78) writing a book on being a successful salesperson
79) writing a book on the effects of drugs on specific diseases
80) writing a book on helping troubled young people

If you were applying for a job, you would likely apply for a position where you . . .
81) could use your strong skills in reading, writing and research
82) could use your strong secretarial related skills
83) were able to do some form of software development
84) could use your skills in drawing/sketching
85) could work directly with customers

A job that would be most satisfying for you would involve . . .
86) some form of creating new technological advances
87) working directly with other people
88) some form of finance and/or banking
89) some form of manual labor
90) caring for the sick and/or elderly

In which of the following situations would you be most helpful . . .
91) building a new addition on a house
92) analyzing trends from market research
93) planning a recreational event for a group
94) helping a customer decide which product was best for him
95) conducting an experiment related to bacteria and viruses

Your community is planning a special event. You could best help by . . .
96) talking to the police or a lawyer regarding the legalities of the event
97) writing an article for a local newspaper after the event
98) organizing a schedule of when things have to be done
99) helping as a computer troubleshooter for the day
100) working as a creative artist in promoting the event

INSTRUCTIONS: In the following section, select the best statement for yourself from each group of five (you must select one answer each time) and print the number of your corresponding answer in the box beside the five statements.

Which of the following would others say you would likely be best at doing . . .
101) helping to resolve customer complaints
102) building a machine that recycles garbage
103) teaching children
104) anything related to mathematics
105) using your hands to make things

Which of the following would others say you would likely be best at doing . . .
106) working in a hospital or other form of health care facility
107) repairing or operating mechanical things
108) promoting a product and/or service
109) helping others to understand nutrition
110) making an effective presentation

Which of the following would you prefer to do . . .
111) attend a workshop on global warming
112) attend a workshop on counseling techniques
113) attend a workshop about a famous author
114) attend a workshop on organizing an office
115) attend a workshop on website security

The greatest personal strength you would bring to a company is . . .
116) your creative talent
117) answering product questions for customers
118) your ability to design solutions for mechanical problems
119) your ability to teach or train others
120) your interest in accounting

In which of the following situations would you be most helpful . . .
121) unloading a truck
122) helping others understand how nutrition affects their health
123) assisting a skilled tradesperson
124) creating an advertisement campaign for a business
125) organizing the catering for an event

INSTRUCTIONS: In the following section, select the best statement for yourself from each group of five (you must select one answer each time) and print the number of your corresponding answer in the box beside the five statements.

Which of the following course areas are of most interest to you . . .

126) marketing, advertising
127) biology, chemistry and/or physics
128) psychology and/or sociology
129) English and/or other languages and/or social sciences
130) office administration

Which of the following course areas are of most interest to you . . .

131) computer operating systems and/or software development
132) art, music and/or drama
133) sales and/or customer services
134) mathematics and/or physics
135) child development and/or human relations

Which of the following course areas are of most interest to you . . .

136) economics and/or finance
137) courses where you work with your hands instead of learning theories
138) courses where you learn about the treatment of injuries and/or diseases
139) courses that lead to apprenticeship opportunities
140) marketing and/or advertising

You could best help a company by . . .

141) developing a lunch recreational program for employees
142) selling their products to potential customers
143) ensuring that environmental standards are being followed
144) arranging child care services for the children of employees
145) translating product manuals into any language other than English

A perfect future job for you would be one where you . . .

146) work as a secretary or as an administrative assistant
147) work with computers and/or other areas of information technology
148) work in a job that lets you express your creative talents
149) work in a job where you are in direct contact with customers
150) work in some form of engineering or a job related to engineering

INSTRUCTIONS: In the following section, select the best statement for yourself from each group of five (you must select one answer each time) and print the number of your corresponding answer in the box beside the five statements.

A perfect future job for you would be one where you . . .

151) work in some form of teaching and/or training others
152) work in a job in the banking or financial services industry
153) work in a job that doesn't require a lot of training or education
154) work in a job related to some form of medical services
155) work in a job using mechanical and/or industrial tools/equipment

A perfect future job for you would be one where you . . .

156) work in a job related to marketing and/or advertising
157) work in a job related to recreation, tourism and/or food services
158) work in a job as a salesperson
159) work in a job where you analyze data from research experiments
160) work in a job helping people who are experiencing personal problems

Congratulations on finishing PART A.
Take a break before you begin PART B.
After you complete PART B,
you will be given further instructions
on how to interpret your results.

INSTRUCTIONS: In the following section, select the best 2 statements for yourself from each group of ten (you must select two answers each time) and print the numbers of your answers in the corresponding boxes beside each group of statements.

If a company was developing a new product you could best help this company by . . .
161) helping to write a product manual
162) assisting an administrator with his/her daily tasks
163) writing a software program to assist in the production
164) creating a song or some form of artwork to celebrate the new product
165) providing services for potential customers
166) being part of the team that is designing the new product
167) keeping the staff informed of what was happening
168) helping to prepare a budget for financing the development
169) helping to keep the factory clean
170) helping to research any possible health issues

You would make the greatest contribution to the building of a bridge if you . . .
171) were involved in the assembly of the structure
172) helped to publicize its benefits to local residents
173) provided either food or recreational services for the workers
174) helped to raise money to finance the project
175) helped to explore the environmental implications of the project
176) helped to organize security on the construction site
177) researched any laws that might affect the project
178) worked in an office to help record the hours worked by each employee
179) set up a teleconferencing network to help coordinate the project
180) created drawings of how the bridge will look when it is finished

If you were applying for a job you would likely apply for a position where you . . .
181) would work directly with the customers
182) worked with structural blueprints
183) could train or teach others
184) were involved in the financial side of the business
185) didn't require a lot of education or training
186) were involved in caring for the health of other people
187) were doing skilled trade work
188) were helping to promote a product or concept
189) were meeting either the leisure or food needs of others
190) would be selling something to the customers

INSTRUCTIONS: In the following section, select the best 2 statements for yourself from each group of ten (you must select two answers each time) and print the numbers of your answers in the corresponding boxes beside each group of statements.

The greatest personal strengths you would bring to a company are . . .

191) your analytical skills in mathematics
192) your strong listening skills
193) your ability to organize a large amount of information
194) your keyboarding skills
195) your skills related to computers and software
196) your artistic talents
197) your ability to resolve conflicts with customers
198) your ability to design solutions for mechanical problems
199) your ability to make presentations to others
200) your analytical skills in financial matters

Which of the following would others say you would do the best . . .

201) use your hands to make things
202) conduct scientific experiments
203) repair and/or operate mechanical things
204) create a logo for a company
205) help others to stay physically fit
206) convince others of your views
207) understand complex scientific concepts
208) help others to resolve their problems
209) write reports or essays
210) perform secretarial related work

In which of the following situations would you be most helpful . . .

211) helping to develop an internet security program
212) being part of a team to develop an animated feature film
213) working with angry customers
214) developing plans for the building of a new machine or mechanical structure
215) helping to tutor kids who are struggling at school
216) assisting someone with their financial planning
217) helping to unload a truck
218) helping to conduct research related to curing cancer
219) helping to landscape the property around a new house
220) helping to analyze trends from market research

INSTRUCTIONS: In the following section, select the best 2 statements for yourself from each group of ten (you must select two answers each time) and print the numbers of your answers in the corresponding boxes beside each group of statements.

Your community is planning a special event. You could best help by . . .

221) organizing either the food services or recreational activities for the event
222) selling tickets for the event
223) providing first aid support for attendees if required
224) talking to the police or a lawyer concerning any legal concerns related to the event
225) writing an article for a local newspaper after the event
226) organizing a schedule of when things have to be done
227) setting up a website for the event
228) entertaining the audience
229) calling potential volunteers to help with the event
230) designing a portable stage to be used for the event

A job that would be most satisfying for you would involve . . .

231) some form of teaching
232) some form of financial services
233) some form of manual labour
234) some form of health care
235) some form of skilled work using tools
236) some form of work in marketing or advertising
237) some form of work in recreation, tourism, or food services
238) some form of selling products or services to others
239) some form of scientific research
240) some form helping special needs children

A job that would be most satisfying for you would involve . . .

241) using your background in languages and/or social sciences
242) doing some form of clerical work and/or administrative assistance
243) working with computers and/or information technology
244) working as a creative artist
245) working in customer services
246) designing or creating new technological advances
247) training other people
248) some form of investment services
249) using your hands to build or construct things
250) caring for sick people

INSTRUCTIONS: In the following section, select the best 2 statements for yourself from each group of ten (you must select two answers each time) and print the numbers of your answers in the corresponding boxes beside each group of statements.

If a company was developing a new product, you could best help this company by . . .
251) helping to actually construct or manufacture the product
252) helping to design the advertising campaign for the product
253) helping to serve lunch for the employees
254) selling the final product to potential customers
255) analyzing the research related to quality control
256) arranging employee assistance program services
257) helping to research any legal concerns related to the new product
258) keyboarding letters for an administrator
259) incorporating the new product information into the company website
260) creating the artwork for the advertising campaign

You would make the greatest contribution to the building of a bridge if you . . .
261) helped at an order desk for purchasing materials
262) helped to assess the structural benefits of various designs
263) helped to present workshops related to employee safety
264) helped to estimate costs for the project
265) helped as a general laborer
266) gave first-aid support to any workers injured on the job
267) used your skills as a tradesperson
268) helped to promote the value of the bridge to the surrounding community
269) helped to organize a banquet for all the workers
270) helped to sell monthly passes for motorists who wanted to use the bridge

If you were applying for a job you would likely apply for a position where you . . .
271) could use your science related skills
272) could help people who have personal problems
273) could use your strong skills in reading, writing, and research
274) could use your office administration skills
275) were able to do some form of software development
276) could use your skills as an artist
277) were helping customers
278) were able to do something related to landscaping
279) were educating others in some way
280) were working in the banking industry in some way

INSTRUCTIONS: In the following section, select the best 2 statements for yourself from each group of ten (you must select two answers each time) and print the numbers of your answers in the corresponding boxes beside each group of statements.

The greatest personal strengths you would bring to a company are . . .
281) your willingness to do any job
282) your interest in preventing work-related diseases
283) your apprenticeship training
284) your creative skills
285) your expertise in organizing social activities
286) your skills in selling
287) your background in scientific research techniques
288) your conflict resolution skills
289) your non-specialized educational background
290) your data entry skills

Which of the following would others say you would do the best . . .
291) repair computers that are not working
292) express yourself artistically
293) answer the telephone in a courteous manner
294) solve mathematical problems
295) help others understand complex topics
296) help others invest in the stock market
297) work in a wide range of jobs that require little education or training
298) help to provide emergency treatment for accident victims
299) repair things when they are broken
300) sell concepts and/or products

In which of the following situations would you be most helpful . . .
301) helping to plan a leisure retreat for a company
302) identifying the needs of customers
303) helping to identify the correct parameters for conducting an experiment
304) helping people to find a job after leaving a correctional facility
305) helping someone understand his/her legal rights
306) organizing the company mail
307) setting up a video-conferencing system for a company
308) being part of a team that is developing a television show
309) helping to clarify company policy for dealing with customer complaints
310) being part of a team that is designing a building complex

INSTRUCTIONS: In the following section, select the best 2 statements for yourself from each group of ten (you must select two answers each time) and print the numbers of your answers in the corresponding boxes beside each group of statements.

Your community is planning a special event. You could best help by . . .

311) training the volunteers
312) keeping a record of expenses
313) helping to set up the stage and chairs
314) providing support for people with special needs
315) setting up the lighting and sound system for the event
316) promoting the event
317) helping to organize travel and hotel arrangements for special guests
318) operating a vending booth of some form at the event
319) researching the risk to the ecology of the proposed site
320) ensuring that the unique needs of elderly people have been considered

Congratulations on finishing PART B.
The next four pages will give you instructions
on how to interpret your results.
On these pages you will begin to see
how your interests relate to possible career choices.

Cherish your visions and your dreams
as they are the child of your soul,
the blueprints of your ultimate achievements.

A SUMMARY OF YOUR INTERESTS

INSTRUCTIONS: On this page and the next page, circle all the numbers that match your answers from pages 14 - 26. After you have circled the numbers, add the number of circles in each column and write this number at the bottom of the appropriate column.

ARTS/ HUMANI-TIES	CLERICAL/ ADMIN. SUPPORT	COMPUT-ERS + INFO. TECH-NOLOGY	CREATIVE ARTS	CUSTOM-ER SER-VICES	DESIGN TECH-NOLOGY	EDUC./ TRAINING	FINAN-CIAL SER-VICES
1	2	3	4	5	6	7	8
17	18	19	20	21	22	23	24
33	34	35	36	37	38	39	40
49	50	51	52	53	54	55	56
65	66	67	68	69	70	71	72
81	82	83	84	85	86	87	88
97	98	99	100	101	102	103	104
113	114	115	116	117	118	119	120
129	130	131	132	133	134	135	136
145	146	147	148	149	150	151	152
161	162	163	164	165	166	167	168
177	178	179	180	181	182	183	184
193	194	195	196	197	198	199	200
209	210	211	212	213	214	215	216
225	226	227	228	229	230	231	232
241	242	243	244	245	246	247	248
257	258	259	260	261	262	263	264
273	274	275	276	277	278	279	280
289	290	291	292	293	294	295	296
305	306	307	308	309	310	311	312

A SUMMARY OF YOUR INTERESTS

INSTRUCTIONS: On this page and the previous page, circle all the numbers that match your answers from pages 14 - 26. After you have circled the numbers, add the number of circles in each column and write this number at the bottom of the appropriate column.

GENERAL HELP	HEALTH CARE/ MEDICAL	MANU-FACTUR-ING + TRADES	MARKET-ING + ADVER-TISING	RECREA-TION + LEISURE	SALES	SCIENCE	SOCIAL/ HELPING SER-VICES
9	10	11	12	13	14	15	16
25	26	27	28	29	30	31	32
41	42	43	44	45	46	47	48
57	58	59	60	61	62	63	64
73	74	75	76	77	78	79	80
89	90	91	92	93	94	95	96
105	106	107	108	109	110	111	112
121	122	123	124	125	126	127	128
137	138	139	140	141	142	143	144
153	154	155	156	157	158	159	160
169	170	171	172	173	174	175	176
185	186	187	188	189	190	191	192
201	202	203	204	205	206	207	208
217	218	219	220	221	222	223	224
233	234	235	236	237	238	239	240
249	250	251	252	253	254	255	256
265	266	267	268	269	270	271	272
281	282	283	284	285	286	287	288
297	298	299	300	301	302	303	304
313	314	315	316	317	318	319	320

ASSESSING YOUR INTERESTS

INTRODUCTION: By completing the following summary you will be able to see your highest career category scores. For some people, these scores will confirm what you have already been thinking about related to your job/career planning. For others, the scores may indicate some new possibilities.

INSTRUCTIONS: List your scores (the number of circles in each column) from pages 27 + 28 beside the appropriate headings below:

ARTS/HUMANITIES = ...

CLERICAL/ADMINISTRATIVE SUPPORT = ...

COMPUTERS/INFORMATION TECHNOLOGY = ...

CREATIVE ARTS = ...

CUSTOMER SERVICES = ...

DESIGN TECHNOLOGY = ...

EDUCATION/TRAINING = ...

FINANCIAL SERVICES = ...

GENERAL HELP = ...

HEALTH CARE/MEDICAL = ...

MANUFACTURING/TRADES = ...

MARKETING/ADVERTISING = ...

RECREATION/LEISURE = ...

SALES = ...

SCIENCE = ...

SOCIAL/HELPING SERVICES = ...

CAREERS THAT BEST MATCH
YOUR INTERESTS

INSTRUCTIONS:

On the top line of CHART A below, list your three highest career category scores from page 29 in order with #1 being your highest score, #2 being your next highest, and #3 being your next highest. If you have any ties, make a decision as to which three areas you think best represent your highest interest categories.

For each of your three highest interest areas, find the matching career list on pages 32 - 47. From each career list, select 3 - 5 careers that you think might be a good match for you and write them in the appropriate columns on CHART A below. A completed sample is provided on the next page in the event you aren't quite sure what to do.

CHART A

1.	2.	3.

SAMPLE

The sample below gives you an idea of how CHART A on page 30 might look when you finish it except that your 3 highest interest categories and career choices will likely be different.

CHART A

1. Financial Services	2. Customer Services	3. Sales
Financial Analyst Stock Broker Financial Planner	Customer Care Specialist Paralegal Sales Representative Real Estate Services	Real Estate Agent Sales Manager Sales Trainer Store Owner

> **"Where your interests meet the needs of this world, there lies your vocation."**
> Aristotle

ARTS/HUMANITIES

ADMINISTRATIVE ASSISTANT
ADVERTISING COPYWRITER
ANTHROPOLOGIST
ARCHAELOGICAL FIELD WORKER
ARCHIVIST
BUYER
CLAIMS ADJUSTER
CLERK
COMMUNICATIONS CONSULTANT
CONSERVATOR
COURT OFFICER
CURATOR
CUSTOMS INSPECTOR
DATA ENTRY CLERK
EDITOR
EDITORIAL ASSISTANT
GEOGRAPHER
HISTORIAN
HUMAN RESOURCES MANAGER
INFORMATION ANALYST
INFORMATION BROKER
INSURANCE AGENT + BROKER
INTERNATIONAL RELATIONS
INTERPRETER
JOURNALIST
LABOUR RELATIONS SPECIALIST
LAW CLERK
LAWYER
LEASING MANAGER
LEGAL ASSISTANT
LIBRARIAN
LIBRARY TECHNICIAN
LOGISTICS DISPATCH PLANNER
MARKET RESEARCHER
NEWS ANALYST

OFFICE ADMINISTRATION
OFFICE ASSISTANT
OFFICE SUPPORT STAFF
ORDER ADMINISTRATOR
PARALEGAL
PLANNER
POLITICAL ORGANIZER
PROOFREADER
PROPERTY ADMINISTRATOR
PROPOSAL WRITER
PUBLIC RELATIONS WORKER
REAL ESTATE BROKER
RESEARCHER
SECRETARY
TEACHER
TOUR GUIDE
TRANSLATOR
TRAVEL AGENT
URBAN PLANNER
WRITER

(FEEL FREE TO ADD ANY OTHER
RELATED CAREERS HERE
THAT YOU MIGHT BE INTERESTED IN)

CLERICAL/ADMINISTRATIVE SUPPORT

ACCOUNT EXECUTIVE
ADMINISTRATIVE SUPPORT
BENEFITS/PAYROLL STAFF
CASHIER
CLAIMS ADJUSTER
CLERK
CLIENT ASSISTANCE
COMPENSATION MANAGER
COST ESTIMATOR
COURT CLERK
CREDIT COLLECTOR
CUSTOMER SERVICES
CUSTOMS BROKER
DATA ENTRY CLERK
DISTRIBUTION ADMINISTRATOR
DISTRIBUTION SERVICES
EXECUTIVE ASSISTANT
INSURANCE REPRESENTATIVE
LAW CLERK
LEASING MANAGER
LEASING SERVICES
LEGAL ASSISTANT
LOAN OFFICER
LOGISTICS DISPATCHER
MAIL ROOM CLERK
MAIL SERVICES MANAGER
MATERIALS BUYER
MEDICAL SECRETARY
OFFICE ADMIN.
OFFICE ASSISTANT
OFFICE SUPPORT STAFF
ORDER ADMINISTRATOR
ORDER CLERK
PACKAGING COORDINATOR

PARTS CLERK
PAYROLL SPECIALIST
PAYROLL/BENEFITS STAFF
PRICING COORDINATOR
PROGRAMMING ASSISTANT
PROPERTY ADMINISTRATOR
PURCHASER
RECEPTIONIST
REPORT PROCESSOR
RESEARCH ASSISTANT
RESEARCHER
SALES SUPPORT
SECRETARY
SENIOR ANALYST
SHIPPING CLERK
SUPPLIER SCHEDULER
TELEMARKETER
TITLE SEARCHER
TRAVEL AGENT

(FEEL FREE TO ADD ANY OTHER
RELATED CAREERS HERE
THAT YOU MIGHT BE INTERESTED IN)

COMPUTERS/INFORMATION TECHNOLOGY

ANALYST
APPLICATIONS ARCHITECT
APPLICATIONS SUPPORT
BUILD ENGINEER
CUSTOMER SERVICES SUPPORT
DATA MODELLER
DATA WAREHOUSING
DESKTOP SUPPORT
DEVELOPMENT SUPPORT
ECOMMERCE ARCHITECT
FILM/VIDEO EDITOR
FIREWARE ENGINEER
GRAPHIC DESIGNER
HTML LAYOUT ASSISTANT
INSTALLATION ENGINEER
INTEGRATION ENGINEER
INTERNET TRAFFIC MANAGER
IT MANAGER
IT PROFESSIONAL
IT SOFTWARE DEVELOPER
JAVA DEVELOPER
JAVA WEB PROGRAMMER
MULTIMEDIA DESIGNER
NET SYSTEMS ARCHITECT
NETWORK ADMIN.
NETWORK OPERATIONS
ORACLE APPLICATIONS
ORACLE DATABASE ARCHITECT
ORACLE PROGRAMMER
PEOPLESOFT DEVELOPER
PEOPLESOFT SPECIALIST
QUALITY CONTROL MANAGER
SAP DEVELOPMENT LEADER

SAP TECHNICAL SUPPORT
SECURITY ANALYST
SENIOR C++ DEVELOPER
SENIOR PROGRAM ANALYST
SOFTWARE BUILDER
SOFTWARE BUSINESS ANALYST
SOFTWARE DEVELOPER
SOFTWARE ENGINEER
SOFTWARE PROGRAMMER
SOFTWARE TESTER
SYSTEMS PROGRAMMER
TEAM LEADER
TECHNICAL ANALYST
TECHNICAL ARCHITECT
TECHNICAL SUPPORT
UNIX ADMINISTRATOR
UNIX SUPPORT
WEB DESIGNER
WEB DEVELOPER
WEBSPHERE SUPPORT
WINDOWS SPECIALIST

(FEEL FREE TO ADD ANY OTHER
RELATED CAREERS HERE
THAT YOU MIGHT BE INTERESTED IN)

CREATIVE ARTS

ACTOR
ADVERTISING DESIGNER
ADVERTISING REPRESENTATIVE
ANIMATOR
ARCHITECT
ARCHITECTURAL TECHNICIAN
ART DEALER
ART DIRECTOR
ARTIST
AUDIO SPECIALIST
AUTHOR
BAKER
CAD TECHNOLOGIST
CAMERA OPERATOR
CARTOONIST
CHAIR UPHOLSTERER
CHOREOGRAPHER
CLOTHING DESIGNER
COSMETICIAN
CREATIVE DIRECTOR
DANCER
DECORATOR
DISPLAY DESIGNER
DRAFTSMAN/WOMAN
FASHION DESIGNER
FILM EDITOR
FILM MAKER
FLORIST
FURNITURE REFINISHER
GALLERY DIRECTOR
GRAPHIC ARTIST
HAIRSTYLIST
ILLUSTRATOR
INTERIOR DECORATOR

MEDIA ADVERTISER
MERCHANDISER
LANDSCAPE ARCHITECT
LIGHTING ARTIST
MODEL
MUSICAL DIRECTOR
MUSICIAN
PHOTOGRAPHER
POTTER
PRODUCER
RECORDING TECHNICIAN
SCRIPT WRITER
SET DESIGNER
SIGN DESIGNER
SINGER
SPECIAL EFFECTS TECHNICIAN
STAGE DIRECTOR
STUDIO MANAGER
TEACHER
VIDEOGRAPHER
WRITER

(FEEL FREE TO ADD ANY OTHER
RELATED CAREERS HERE
THAT YOU MIGHT BE INTERESTED IN)

CUSTOMER SERVICES

ACCOUNT MANAGER
ACCOUNT SERVICES
ACCOUNTS RECEIVABLE
ADMINISTRATIVE ASSISTANCE
ASSET RECOVERY SPECIALIST
CALL CENTER AGENT
CALL CENTER MANAGEMENT
CASHIER
CLERK
COLLECTION REPRESENTATIVE
COMMUNICATIONS AGENT
COMMUNITY SALES ASSOCIATE
CREDIT ANALYST
CUSTOMER CARE ASSOCIATE
CUSTOMER CARE SPECIALIST
CUSTOMER CONTACT AGENT
CUSTOMER SERVICE ASSOCIATE
CUSTOMER SERVICES CLERK
CUSTOMER SERVICES
DATA ENTRY CLERK
DIRECTOR OF OPERATIONS
DISPATCHER
EMPLOYEE RELATIONS OFFICER
FIELD TECHNICIAN
FINANCIAL CUSTOMER SERVICE
HELP DESK AGENT
INBOUND CUSTOMER SERVICE
INBOUND INFORMATION AGENT
LOAN OFFICER
MARKET RESEARCH
OFFICE ASSISTANT
OPERATIONS MANAGER
ORDER CLERK
ORDER DESK REPRESENTATIVE

ORDER DESK SPECIALIST
PARALEGAL
PRODUCT COORDINATOR
QUALITY ASSURANCE MANAGER
REAL ESTATE SERVICES
RECEPTIONIST
RECRUITER
RETAIL SALESPERSON
ROUTE SALES REPRESENTATIVE
SALES ASSOCIATE
SALES REPRESENTATIVE
SECRETARY
SERVICE COORDINATOR
SERVICE MANAGER
STAFFING CONSULTANT
SUPPORT ASSISTANCE
TECHNICAL SUPPORT AGENT
TELEMARKETER
TELEPHONE INTERVIEWER
TELEPHONE SALES AGENT
TELESALES TRAINING DIRECTOR

(FEEL FREE TO ADD ANY OTHER
RELATED CAREERS HERE
THAT YOU MIGHT BE INTERESTED IN)

DESIGN TECHNOLOGY

AEROSPACE ENGINEER
APPLICATIONS ENGINEER
APPLICATIONS SUPPORT
ARCHITECT
ARCHITECTURAL TECHNICIAN
AUTOMOTIVE DESIGNER
AUTOMOTIVE ENGINEER
CAD TECHNICIAN
CHEMICAL ENGINEER
CIVIL ENGINEER
CNC OPERATOR-MACHINIST
CNC PROGRAMMER
COMPUTER PROGRAMMER
CONTROLS ENGINEER
DESIGN ENGINEER
DIE CAST DESIGNER
DRAFTSPERSON
DRAFTING TECHNICIAN
ELECTRICAL DESIGNER
ELECTRICAL TECHNOLOGIST
ENGINEERING TECHNICIAN
ENVIRONMENTAL ENGINEER
FIELD ENGINEER
FITTER
GEOLOGICAL ENGINEER
INDUSTRIAL DESIGNER
INSTRUMENTATION DESIGNER
INTERIOR DESIGNER
JOURNEYMAN/WOMAN
LANDSCAPE ARCHITECT
MECHANICAL ENGINEER
MILLWRIGHT
MINING ENGINEER
QUALITY INSPECTOR

MULTIMEDIA/INTERFACE ARTIST
NUCLEAR ENGINEER
PLAN EXAMINER
PROCESS ENGINEER
PRODUCT DESIGNER
QUALITY CONTROL ANALYST
RESEARCH ENGINEER
ROBOT PROGRAMMER
ROBOTICS DESIGNER
ROBOTICS ENGINEER
SOLUTIONS ARCHITECT
STATIONARY ENGINEER
STRUCTURAL STEEL DETAILER
TECHNICAL WRITER
TELECOM ANALYST
TEST ENGINEER
TOOL DESIGNER
TOOL ENGINEER
WEB ARCHITECT
WEB DESIGNER
WELDING ENGINEER

(FEEL FREE TO ADD ANY OTHER
RELATED CAREERS HERE
THAT YOU MIGHT BE INTERESTED IN)

EDUCATION/TRAINING

ADMINISTRATOR
CAMP PROGRAM LEADER
CAREER ADVISOR
CAREER COUNSELOR
CHILD CARE WORKER
CHILD SUPPORT WORKER
CLINICAL INSTRUCTOR
CORPORATE EXECUTIVE
COUNSELOR
COURSE DEVELOPER
COURSE TESTER
CURRICULUM DESIGNER
CUSTOMER SERVICES TRAINER
DAY CARE WORKER
EARLY CHILDHOOD EDUCATOR
EMPLOYMENT COUNSELOR
GERIATRIC INSTRUCTOR
HEALTH & SAFETY MANAGER
HUMAN RESOURCES SPECIALIST
INSTRUCTOR
LABOUR RELATIONS MANAGER
LABOUR RELATIONS SPECIALIST
NURSERY SCHOOL TEACHER
ONLINE TEACHER
ORGANIZATIONAL DEVELOPER
PERSONNEL MANAGER
POLICE OFFICER
PROFESSIONAL SPEAKER
PROFESSOR
PROGRAM DIRECTOR
PROJECT MANAGER
PSYCHIATRIST

RECRUITER
RECRUITMENT CONSULTANT
RECRUITMENT MANAGER
RESEARCHER
RETENTION DIRECTOR
SCHOOL ADMINISTRATOR
STAFFING CONSULTANT
STAFFING COORDINATOR
STAFFING SERVICES
STAFFING SPECIALIST
TEACHER
TEACHER AIDE
TEACHER ASSISTANT
TRAINER
TRAINING COORDINATOR
TRAINING SPECIALIST
TUTOR
WORKSHOP ASSISTANT
WORKSHOP LEADER
WRITER
YOUTH COUNSELOR

(FEEL FREE TO ADD ANY OTHER
RELATED CAREERS HERE
THAT YOU MIGHT BE INTERESTED IN)

FINANCIAL SERVICES

ACCOUNT MANAGER
ACCOUNTANT
ACCOUNTING ASSISTANT
ACCOUNTING CLERK
ACCOUNTING SUPERVISOR
ACCOUNTING TECHNICIAN
ACCOUNTS PAYABLE
ACCOUNTS RECEIVABLE
ACTUARY
APPRAISER
AUDITOR
BAD DEBT RECOVERY MANAGER
BANK OPERATIONS MANAGER
BANK TELLER
BANKING OFFICER
BOOKKEEPER
BRANCH MANAGER
BUDGET MANAGER
BUSINESS ANALYST
CHIEF FINANCIAL OFFICER
CALL CENTRE
CLAIMS OFFICER
COMPTROLLER/CONTROLLER
CONTRACT ADMINISTRATOR
COST ANALYST
CREDIT MANAGER
DIRECT BANKING ASSOCIATE
DIRECTOR OF FINANCE
ECONOMIST
FINANCIAL ANALYST
FINANCIAL COUNSULTANT
FINANCIAL PLANNER
FINANCIAL SERVICES
INSURANCE ADJUSTER

INSURANCE SERVICES
INVESTMENT ADVISOR
INVESTMENT BANKER
LEASING SERVICES
LOAN MANAGER
MERCHANDISING MANAGER
MORTGAGE SPECIALIST
MUTUAL FUNDS SALES
PAYROLL OFFICER
POINT-OF-SALES ANALYST
PORTFOLIO MANAGER
PRICING ANALYST
RISK ANALYST
SECURITIES ANALYST
SECURITIES DEALER
STOCK BROKER
TAX SPECIALIST
TREASURER
TREASURY ANALYST/MANAGER
TRUST OPPORTUNITIES
UNDERWRITER

(FEEL FREE TO ADD ANY OTHER
RELATED CAREERS HERE
THAT YOU MIGHT BE INTERESTED IN)

GENERAL HELP

AGRICULTURAL WORKER
ANIMAL CARE HELPER
ASSEMBLER
ASSEMBLY LINE WORKER
BANQUET SERVER
BUILDING SUPERINTENDENT
CARETAKER
CASHIER
CATERING HELP
CLEANING SERVICES
CLERK
CONSTRUCTION WORKER
COOK
DELIVERY DRIVER
DISHWASHER
DRIVERS
EVENT STAFF
FARM WORKER
FAST FOOD SERVICES
FISHING WORKER
FLYER DISTRIBUTOR
FOOD SERVICES WORKER
FORESTRY WORKER
GENERAL LABOURER
HAIRSTYLIST
HOME CARE WORKER
HOME DELIVERY SERVICES
HOUSEKEEPING SERVICES
INSTALLER
KITCHEN HELP
LANDSCAPE WORKER
MAINTENANCE SERVICES
MINING SERVICES

NURSERY WORKER
ORDER ASSEMBLER
PACKERS
PAINTER
PARK WORKER
PICKERS
PRODUCTION WORKER
RAILWAY WORKER
RECREATION FACILITY AT-
TENDANT
RECREATION FACILITY MAINTE-
NANCE
RESTAURANT SERVICES
RETAIL SALES CLERK
SANITATION WORKER
SERVICE TECHNICIAN
SHIPPER/RECEIVER
SHIPPING COORDINATOR
STOCK PERSON
TELEMARKETER
TRUCK DRIVER
WAITER/WAITRESS

(FEEL FREE TO ADD ANY OTHER
RELATED CAREERS HERE
THAT YOU MIGHT BE INTERESTED IN)

HEALTH CARE/MEDICAL

ACUPUNCTURIST
ADDICTION SERVICES
AUDIOLOGIST
BIOSTATISTICIAN
CARDIOLOGY
CASE MANAGER
CHIROPRACTOR
CLINICAL DATA MANAGER
CLINICAL NURSE
CLINICAL RESEARCHER
DENTAL ASSISTANT
DENTAL HYGIENIST
DERMATOLOGIST
DIETITIAN/NUTRITIONIST
DRUG SAFETY INSTRUCTOR
FOOD SAFETY AUDITOR
GERIATRICIAN
HEALTH CARE ANALYST
HEALTH CARE CONSULTANT
HOME CARE WORKER
KINESIOLOGIST
MASSAGE THERAPIST
MEDICAL LAB TECHNICIAN
MEDICAL RECORDS KEEPER
MEDICAL SECRETARY
NUCLEAR MEDICINE
NURSE
NURSE CLINICIAN
NURSE PRACTITIONER
OBSTETRICIAN
OCCUPATIONAL HEALTH NURSE
OCCUPATIONAL THERAPIST

OPTICIAN
OPTOMETRIST
PALLIATIVE CARE
PARAMEDIC
PATHOLOGIST
PHARMACIST
PHARMACOLOGIST
PHARMACY TECHNICIAN
PHYSICAL THERAPIST
PHYSICIAN
PSYCHIATRIC NURSE
PSYCHIATRIST
PUBLIC HEALTH NURSE
REHABILITATION COUNSELOR
RESEARCH SCIENTIST
SLEEP DISORDER SERVICES
SPEECH PATHOLOGIST
SURGEON
ULTRASOUND TECHNOLOGIST
VET ASSISTANT
VETERINARIAN

(FEEL FREE TO ADD ANY OTHER
RELATED CAREERS HERE
THAT YOU MIGHT BE INTERESTED IN)

MANUFACTURING/TRADES

ALARM TECHNICIAN
ASSEMBLER
AUTOMOTIVE INSTALLER
AUTOMOTIVE STAMPER
BELT FABRICATOR
BLOW MOULDING MANAGER
BUILDING MAINTENANCE TECHNI-
CIAN
CABINET MAKER
CAD OPERATOR
CAD TECHNICIAN
CARPENTER
CHIEF BOILER
CNC MACHINE OPERATOR
CONSTRUCTION MANAGER
CONSTRUCTION WORKER
DIESEL TECHNICIAN
DOCK FOREMAN
DRIVER
ELECTRICAL TECHNICIAN
ELECTRICIAN
FACILITY TECHNICIAN
FINISHER
FLAT GLASS GLAZIER
FORKLIFT OPERATOR
HEAVY DUTY EQUIPMENT OPERA-
TOR
INSTALLATION WORKER
INSTRUMENTATION MECHANIC
JOURNEYMAN/WOMAN
LASER SYSTEMS OPERATOR
MAINTENANCE TECHNICIAN
MANUFACTURING SUPERVISOR

MECHANIC
METAL WORKER
MILLWRIGHT
OPERATIONS MANAGER
PLANT MANAGER
PLUMBER
PRESS OPERATOR
PROCESS MANAGER
PRODUCTION WORKER
QUALITY CONTROL TECHNICIAN
REFRIGERATION SPECIALIST
REPAIR SERVICES
ROBOT TECHNICIAN
SECURITY TECHNICIAN
SERVICE SPECIALIST
SHIFT SUPERVISOR
SHIPPER/RECEIVER
TECHNICAL SUPPORT
TECHNICIAN
TOOLING DESIGNERS
WAREHOUSE MANAGER
WAREHOUSE WORKER

(FEEL FREE TO ADD ANY OTHER
RELATED CAREERS HERE
THAT YOU MIGHT BE INTERESTED IN)

MARKETING/ADVERTISING

ACCOUNT MANAGER
ADVERTISING CONSULTANT
ADVERTISING MANAGER
ADVERTISING SALES
ART/CREATIVE DIRECTOR
BRAND MARKETER
BUSINESS ANALYST
BUYER
CHIEF CREATIVE OFFICER
CHIEF EXECUTIVE OFFICER
COMMERCIAL PRICING ANALYST
COMMUNICATIONS SPECIALIST
CONFERENCE DEVELOPER
CONFERENCE PLANNER
CONSULTANT
COPYWRITER
DESKTOP PUBLISHER
DIRECT MARKETING MANAGER
DIRECTOR OF DESIGN
DISPLAY MARKETER
E-COMMERCE SPECIALIST
EVENT & PROMOTION STAFF
EVENT MARKETING
EVENT PRODUCER
GRAPHIC ARTIST
GRAPHIC DESIGNER
MARKET RESEARCHER
MARKETING ANALYST
MARKETING MANAGER
MEDIA BUYER
MEDIA PLANNER
MERCHANDISER

ON-LINE MARKETING MANAGER
PACKAGE DESIGNER
PRICING ANALYST
PRINT PRODUCTION MANAGER
PRODUCT MANAGER
PROJECT MANAGER
PRICING ANALYST
PUBLIC RELATIONS ADVISOR
RENEWAL MARKETING MANAGER
RETAIL SALES
SALES PROFESSIONAL
SENIOR MARKETING SPECIALIST
SOFTWARE PRODUCT MARKETING
SPECIAL EVENTS & PROMOTIONS
TELEMARKETER
TELEPHONE SALES
VISUAL MERCHANDISER
VISUAL PRESENTATION MANAGER
WEB MARKETER
WEB MARKETING CONSULTANT
WRITER

(FEEL FREE TO ADD ANY OTHER
RELATED CAREERS HERE
THAT YOU MIGHT BE INTERESTED IN)

RECREATION/LEISURE

ANNOUNCER
ATHLETE
ATHLETE TRAINER
BANQUET MANAGER
BANQUET SERVER
CAMP COORDINATOR
CASINO ATTENDANT
CHEF
CONVENTION MANAGER
CORPORATE TRAVEL AGENT
CRUISE SHIP WORKER
ENTERTAINER
EVENT MANAGER
FITNESS CONSULTANT
FITNESS INSTRUCTOR
FLIGHT SERVICES
FOOD + BEVERAGES SERVICES
FOOD SERVICES MANAGER
GOLF PRO
GUEST SERVICES MANAGER
HOTEL SERVICES
HOUSEKEEPING SERVICES
KINESIOLOGIST
KITCHEN MANAGER
LEISURE CONSULTANT
LIFEGUARD
LIFESTYLE PLANNER
PARK RANGER
PARK WORKER
PUBLIC RELATIONS SPECIALIST
PUBLIC RELATIONS WORKER
RECREATION DIRECTOR

RECREATION INSTRUCTOR
RECREATION PLANNER
REFEREE/UMPIRE
RESORT MANAGER
RESORT STAFF
RESTAURANT MANAGER
RETIREMENT COUNSELOR
SALES REPRESENTATIVE
SPA POOL SERVICES
SPORT PSYCHOLOGIST
SPORTS CONSULTANT
SPORTS EDITOR
SPORTS PHYSICIAN
SPORTS WRITER
TEACHER
TENNIS PRO
TICKET SALES
TOUR GUIDE
TOUR OPERATOR
TRAVEL AGENT
TRAVEL GUIDE
TRAVEL WRITER
WAITER/WAITRESS

(FEEL FREE TO ADD ANY OTHER
RELATED CAREERS HERE
THAT YOU MIGHT BE INTERESTED IN)

SALES

ACCOUNT MANAGER
AGENCY DIRECTOR
APPLIANCE SALESPERSON
ASSISTANT STORE MANAGER
BUSINESS DEVELOPMENT
BUYER
COMMERCIAL PRODUCTS
CORPORATE ACCOUNTS
CUSTOMER SERVICES
DIRECT SALES PROFESSIONAL
DIRECTOR OF MARKETING
DISTRICT SALES MANAGER
ENTRY LEVEL MANAGEMENT
EQUIPMENT SALES MANAGER
FIELD SALES MANAGER
FIELD SERVICES
FINANCIAL CONSULTANT
FINANCIAL SERVICES MANAGER
GENERAL MANAGER
INDUSTRIAL SALES
INSURANCE AGENT
INSURANCE SALES
INTERNET SALES .
INVESTMENT DEALER
LEASING ADMINISTRATOR
MERCHANDISER
MORTGAGE SPECIALIST
NEW ACCOUNT DEVELOPMENT
OUTBOUND CALL CENTER SALES
POINT OF PURCHASE DISPLAY
PRODUCT SPECIALIST
REAL ESTATE AGENT

REAL ESTATE BROKER
REGIONAL SALES MANAGER
RENTAL OPERATIONS MANAGER
RESP SPECIALIST
RETAIL SALES PERSON
RETAIL STORE SUPERVISOR
SALES ANALYST
SALES CONSULTANT
SALES ENGINEER
SALES EXECUTIVE
SALES MANAGER
SALES PROFESSIONAL
SALES REPRESENTATIVE
SALES TRAINER
SERVICE DELIVERY SPECIALIST
STORE OWNER
STRATEGIC ACCOUNT MANAGER
TELEMARKETER
TELESALES MANAGER
TELESALES REPRESENTATIVE
VISUAL MERCHANDISING
WAITER/WAITRESS
WINDOW STYLIST

(FEEL FREE TO ADD ANY OTHER
RELATED CAREERS HERE
THAT YOU MIGHT BE INTERESTED IN)

SCIENCE

AGRICULTURAL PROFESSIONAL
ANALYST
ANIMAL CARE TECHNICIAN
ASSOCIATE SCIENTIST
BIOANALYTICAL POSITIONS
BIOCHEMIST
BIOMEDICAL ENGINEER
BIOSTATISTICIAN
CHEMIST
CLINICAL DATA MANAGER
CLINICAL RESEARCHER
CLINICAL SCIENTIST
ECOLOGICAL SCIENTIST
EMBRYOLOGIST
ENGINEER
FARM SUPERVISOR
FOOD SCIENTIST
FORENSIC CHEMIST
FORMULATION RESEARCHER
HYDROGEOLOGIST
LAB SUPERVISOR
LAB TECHNICIAN
MARINE BIOLOGIST
MATERIALS SCIENTIST
MEDICAL LAB TECHNICIAN
MEDICAL WRITER
MICROBIOLOGIST
NURSE
OCCUPATIONAL HYGIENIST
OCCUPATIONAL THERAPIST
PACKAGING RESEARCHER
PHARMACIST

PHARMACOLOGIST
PHYSICAL THERAPIST
PHYSICIAN
PRODUCT DEVELOPER
PROFESSOR
PROJECT LEADER
PROJECT SCIENTIST
QUALITY ASSURANCE AUDITOR
QUALITY CONTROL TECHNICIAN
QUALITY SYSTEMS ASSOCIATE
R + D SUPERVISOR
REGULATORY SCIENTIST
RESEARCH ASSISTANT
RESEARCHER
SCIENTIST
SUPERVISOR OF RESEARCH
TEACHER
TECHNICIAN
VETERINARIAN
VETERINARIAN ASSISTANT
WATER QUALITY RESEARCHER
X-RAY TECHNICIAN
ZOOLOGIST

(FEEL FREE TO ADD ANY OTHER
RELATED CAREERS HERE
THAT YOU MIGHT BE INTERESTED IN)

SOCIAL/HELPING SERVICES

ADDICTIONS COUNSELOR
AMBULANCE ATTENDANT
CAREER ADVISOR
CAREER COUNSELOR
CHILD AND YOUTH WORKER
CHIROPRACTOR AIDE
COMMUNITY YOUTH WORKER
CORRECTIONAL OFFICER
COUNSELOR
CUSTOMER SERVICES
DAY CARE WORKER
DENTAL ASSISTANT
DIETICIAN
EMPLOYMENT COUNSELOR
FIREFIGHTER
FLIGHT SERVICES
FUNERAL SERVICES
GERIATRIC WORKER
HAIRSTYLIST
HOME HEALTH AIDE
HUMAN RESOURCES MANAGER
INDUSTRIAL RELATIONS
INSTRUCTOR
JUDGE
LABOUR RELATIONS SPECIALIST
LAWYER
LEGAL ASSISTANT
MASSAGE THERAPIST
NANNY
NURSE
NURSE AIDE
OCCUPATIONAL THERAPIST
ORDERLY

PARALEGAL
PARAMEDIC
PERSONAL SUPPORT WORKER
PERSONNEL MANAGER
PHYSIOTHERAPIST
PHYSIOTHERAPIST ASSISTANT
POLICE OFFICER
PRIVATE INVESTIGATOR
PROBATION OFFICER
PSYCHIATRIC AIDE
PSYCHIATRIST
PSYCHOLOGIST
PUBLIC RELATIONS AGENT
RECREATION LEADER
REHABILITATION SERVICES
SECURITY GUARD
SERVICE MANAGER
SOCIAL WORKER
SPECIAL NEEDS WORKER
SPEECH PATHOLOGIST
TEACHER
TRAUMA COUNSELOR

(FEEL FREE TO ADD ANY OTHER
RELATED CAREERS HERE
THAT YOU MIGHT BE INTERESTED IN)

"If we all did the things we are capable of, we would astound ourselves."

Thomas A. Edison

IDENTIFYING YOUR ABILITIES

While identifying the things you are interested in is an important step in discovering the perfect career for you, it is equally important to understand which things you can do well. You might love football and dream of being a professional football player, but unless you have the required ability to play football, then it is unlikely that this dream will come true. Similarly, you might have a strong interest in being an elementary or high school teacher, but once again without the ability to complete the required education, this interest will not transpire into reality.

When love and ability work together, expect a masterpiece.

When your natural abilities support what you are interested in, this becomes a perfect marriage for success. People who achieve the greatest success in their careers generally spend most of their time doing the things they are best at. For most of us, as we go through school (and life), we are often reminded of our weaknesses. We are often told to work on our weaknesses. Unfortunately, such an approach can prevent you from enhancing your strengths. Identifying your strengths (your strongest interests and abilities) and focusing your efforts on enhancing these increases your likelihood of achieving success in your career choice.

Over time, and through various forms of education, training, life experiences and actual job experiences, your abilities eventually translate into the building of skills.

For the purpose of this book, skills will be categorized as either "personal" or "job specific".

In this chapter, you will have an opportunity to identify your unique abilities as demonstrated by your personal skills and job related skills. Once you better understand your abilities and skills you can better select a career that allows you to build on these strengths.

Unfortunately, some people never take the time to discovery these abilities, and as a result never find the career that is perfect for them. In these situations, people continually struggle in their daily jobs because what they are doing is not easy for them. They constantly feel uncomfortable and even inadequate. On the other hand, people who have clearly identified their abilities and choose careers that give them the opportunity to best use these talents find greater job satisfaction. Identifying your abilities and skills can help give focus to your search in finding the perfect career.

Doing what you do best is generally a solid recipe for success.

"The trick is in what we emphasize.
We either make ourselves miserable,
or we make ourselves strong.
The amount of work is the same."
Carlos Castaneda

YOUR ABILITIES

INSTRUCTIONS: Answer the following questions. It is okay to repeat the same answer for different questions.

1. What is something that you love to do because you are good at doing it?

2. What is something that others tell you are good at doing?

3. What is something that you can do that you think you can do better than most other people?

4. What is something that you love to do so much that you would consider doing it even if you did not receive any money for doing it?

5. If you were attending some form of school during the next year and you could take only one subject, what subject would you choose?

6. What is something you would love to do every day (not including weekends) for the next five years?

7. If you were asked to identify an ability/talent that you have that just seems to come naturally for you, what would it be?

SUMMARY

From your answers above, identify two things that you are really good at doing.

1.

2.

IDENTIFYING YOUR PERSONAL SKILLS

SOME SAMPLE PERSONAL SKILLS

The following provides some examples of personal skills. If you have any personal skills that are not included in this list, then add them at the end of the list.

- adaptable
- ambitious
- analytical
- assertive
- calm
- confident
- courteous
- creative
- dependable
- empathetic
- focused
- goal orientated
- honest
- independent
- leader
- likes to learn
- logical
- organized
- persuasive
- positive
- practical
- problem solver
- punctual
- quick learner
- self-motivated
- team player

YOUR PERSONAL SKILLS

From the list on the left hand side of this page (including any personal skills you added to the list), identify your top five personal skills and write them below with #1 being your strongest personal skill, #2 your next strongest, and so on.

1. . . . .

2. . . . .

3. . . . .

4. . . . .

5. . . . .

IDENTIFYING YOUR JOB SPECIFIC SKILLS

SOME SAMPLE JOB SPECIFIC SKILLS

The following provides some examples of job specific skills. If you have any job specific skills that are not included in this list, then add them at the end of the list.

- assemble equipment
- AZ licence
- bilingual
- can read blueprints + schematics
- computer proficient
- proficient with Microsoft Office
- skilled with hand tools
- strong writing skills
- proficient in web technology
- proven sales ability
- maintain inventory records
- troubleshoot mechanical problems
- installation skills
- accounting skills
- instrumentation skills
- record keeping skills
- writing project proposals
- construction experience
- software design skills
- repair machinery

YOUR JOB SPECIFIC SKILLS

From the list on the left hand side of this page (including any job specific skills you added to the list), identify your top five job specific skills and write them below with #1 being your strongest skill, #2 your next strongest, and so on.

1. . . . .

2. . . . .

3. . . . .

4. . . . .

5. . . . .

A SUMMARY OF YOUR ABILITIES/SKILLS

In this chapter you have been considering your abilities and skills. The following chart provides an opportunity for you to summarize your top abilities and skills.

CHART B

List the 2 abilities you stated at the bottom of page 51 . . .

    1)

    2)

Identify your top 3 "personal skills" from page 52 . . .

    1)

    2)

    3)

Identify your top 3 "job specific skills" from page 53 . . .

    1)

    2)

    3)

ANOTHER LOOK AT MY FUTURE PLANS

INSTRUCTIONS:

On CHART C below, list any careers from CHART A on page 30 that would require some of the abilities and skills you identified on CHART B on page 54. In other words which careers depend on the abilities and skills that you listed on page 54? It might be useful for you to consult with a coach, counselor or career advisor to help you with this.

In addition, take a look once again at all the careers listed on pages 32 - 47 and select any additional careers that require the abilities and skills that you listed on page 54. Add these careers as well to CHART C below.

CHART C

THE TOP CAREERS I AM INTERESTED IN
(based on my interests and abilities)

**Happiness comes from
doing what you believe in.**

IDENTIFYING YOUR VALUES

To a very large degree, your values will determine your job satisfaction. To be really happy in a career, you need to align your values with what you are doing. For example, a person who values working in the outdoors will not be happy working in an indoor small office day after day, year after year. Similarly, a person who values helping other people will not gain lasting satisfaction from filing papers in an office day after day, year after year. The most successful people love what they do and do what they love. Your values play an important role in determining what it is that you love to do.

What then is a value? A dictionary would define a value as:

- the importance of a thing
- the relative rank or importance
- what something is worth
- the usefulness of something
- something you hold dear to you
- something you cherish
- something you regard highly and respect

A thesaurus would use some of the following words to describe value:

- worth, benefit, advantage
- importance, merit, significance
- usefulness, worthiness

The most successful people love what they do and do what they love.

When you find the best career for you, you will wake up excited each day about what you are going to be doing.

Ask yourself the following questions:

1) What is really important to you?
2) What is something you cherish about yourself?
3) What are some things that you do that you really love doing?

Many people divide their time between what they have to do to earn a living and what they do to have fun. Real career satisfaction comes from knowing what makes you feel good about yourself and integrating this into your career selection. The best career for you will simply be an extension of who you are in your life away from the workplace. A career that arouses your passions will contribute to your happiness.

In order to find such a career, first of all you have to identify your values. By being aware of what is most important to you, it is much easier to find the career that is best for you. If you don't take the time to first identify your values, you might end up in a career, like so many others, that was based on what you thought your parents wanted you to do, or what a teacher/counselor told you you would be good at, or you simply jumped at the first job that became available because it was easy to get into, or the pay (at that time) appeared to be good.

A list of values (and a brief description of each value) that are often identified as being part of career choice is provided on the next few pages. The values are listed in alphabetical order. As you read each value and description, begin to think about which of the values are most important to you.

ADVANCEMENT: you would like the opportunity to rise or be promoted to increasing levels of expertise, management or leadership within a company or organization.

CHALLENGE: you would like a career that offers challenges for you each day. This is a job where you will need to constantly keep learning in order to be able to handle new projects that you are involved in each day.

COMPETITIVE: you would like a career where you are competing against others as part of your job. You enjoy the prospect of constantly trying to be the best in reaching your own goals or in comparison to other people or even companies.

CREATIVE EXPRESSION: you would like a career that offers an opportunity for you to be very creative. This would tend to be job where you can best employ your artistic talents or be inventive.

ENTREPRENEURIAL: you would like a career that offers you the opportunity to do things your way (preferably to start your own business). You tend to enjoy taking risks and you are very good at promoting what you do.

FOLLOWER: you would like a career where someone tells you each day exactly what you have to do and how to do it. Your job would be to primarily follow instructions rather than create new ways of doing things.

HELP OTHERS: you would like a career where you are given the opportunity to make a difference in the lives of others.

HIGH EARNINGS: you would like a career where you have the opportunity to make a lot of money.

INDEPENDENCE: you would like a career where you have the freedom to choose when and how you want to work. This job would give you the flexibility to choose what you want to do each day.

"Many people have the wrong idea of what constitutes true happiness. It is not attained through self-gratification but through devotion to a worthy purpose."
Helen Keller

Every decision we make is a reflection of our values.

KNOWLEDGE: you would like a career where you are constantly learning. Your job allows you to work in research and the development of new ideas and possibilities.

LEADERSHIP: you would like a career where you have the opportunity to be a leader. You like to influence others and be in charge.

PHYSICAL CHALLENGE: you would like a career where there is a strong physical component to what you do each day.

PRACTICAL: you would like a career where what you do each day is very practical and at the end of the day you can actually see something concrete that you have made, developed or designed.

PRECISE: you would like a career where your work depends on attention to detail.

PRESTIGE: you would like a career where you feel the job is looked upon by others as being prestigious giving you more status in the eyes of yourself and others.

PROBLEM SOLVING: you would like a career where each day there are problems and challenges to solve or resolve.

PUBLIC CONTACT: you would like a career that offers you the opportunity to meet new people each day such as customers and/or clients.

RECOGNITION: you would like a career where you receive recognition and/or respect from others, whether it is a from strangers, or from the people you work with.

SERVICE: you would like a career where you assist other people in getting what they want and/or need.

SPIRITUALITY: you would like a career where you work each day with people who have the same spiritual beliefs as you or where you have the opportunity to share your spiritual beliefs with others.

STRUCTURE: you would like a career where there is a set structure and predictability to what you do each day. You tend not to like change.

TEAMWORK: you would like a career where you are often working as part of a team with other people. You like to share ideas with others and work together on projects or assignments.

VARIETY: you would like a career where there is constant variety in what you do each day. You look forward to doing something different each day.

WORK-LIFE BALANCE: you would like a career that provides an opportunity to balance your time with family, hobbies, or other interests with the time necessary to work in your job.

WORLD BETTERMENT: you would like a career where you have the opportunity to make this world a better place to live.

OTHER: perhaps, there is a value, or even values, that are important to you that have not been listed above. If so, write this value or values in the space below.

Choose your own career path, otherwise someone else may choose the wrong one for you.

IDENTIFYING YOUR CORE VALUES

**Be true
to yourself.**

On the past few pages you have had the opportunity to read a brief description of some of the values that can affect career selection and satisfaction. The values that are most important to you are not necessarily the ones that are most important to others. By identifying the values that are most important to you, you are taking another step in finding the career that is best for you.

As you begin to identify your core values, it is critical to identify the values that you feel most comfortable with. Choosing values because you think they are the ones that others expect of you may lead you in the wrong direction. I have counseled some very unhappy people who stayed in a miserable job year after year because their parents, or relatives, or a teacher, or a friend once told them this was the best career path for them.

Choose your own career path, otherwise someone else might choose the wrong one for you. Yes, it is important to get feedback from your family, teachers, and friends, but ultimately it is your choice.

**Failing to plan
carefully
for your future
is unfortunately
planning
to fail.**

On the next page, identify your top five values from pages 59 - 61 (including any that you wrote yourself on the bottom of page 61). It would likely be helpful to you to read all the values on these pages once again to familiarize yourself with them. In fact, most people will have to re-read these lists several times in order to identify their top five values. In identifying your top five values, write them in priority order with #1 being your top value, #2 your next most important, and so on. Remember, you are selecting the values that are most important to you, not the ones you think others want you to list.

THE VALUES THAT ARE MOST IMPORTANT TO YOU

INSTRUCTIONS

In the spaces below, list the five values from pages 59 - 61 that are most important to you. Write these in priority order with #1 being the most important to you, #2 being the next most important, and so on. By taking your time and selecting these five values very carefully, you will be taking another step in understanding which career is best for you.

MY TOP FIVE VALUES

1. . . . .

2. . . . .

3. . . . .

4. . . . .

5. . . . .

advancement
challenge
competitive
creative expression
entrepreneurial
follower
help others
high earnings
independence
knowledge
leadership
physical challenge
practical
precise
prestige
problem solving
public contact
recognition
service
spirituality
structure
teamwork
variety
work-life balance
world betterment
other

> **"Happiness is when what you think,
> what you say,
> and what you do
> are in harmony."**
> Gandhi

APPLYING MY VALUES TO MY CAREER CHOICES

INSTRUCTIONS:

Look once again at the careers that you wrote on CHART C on page 55. As you read your list of careers, ask yourself which of these careers best match your top five values from page 63. Write any of these careers on CHART D below.

CHART D

MY TOP CAREERS
(based on my interests, abilities/skills and values)

WHAT SOME FAMOUS PEOPLE HAVE SAID ABOUT FINDING THE PERFECT CAREER

"It is more important to know where you are going
than to get there quickly."
Mabel Newcomber

"Just don't give up trying to do what you really want to do.
Where there is love and inspiration, I don't think you can go wrong."
Ella Fitzgerald

"Failure is an opportunity to more intelligently begin again."
Henry Ford

"Pleasure in the job puts perfection in the work."
Aristotle

"In the long run you only hit what you aim at."
Henry David Thoreau

"Growth itself contains the germ of happiness."
Pearl S. Buck

"There's no scarcity of opportunity to make a living at what you love.
There is only a scarcity of resolve to make it happen."
Dr. Wayne Dyer

"Step by step.
I can't think of any other way of accomplishing anything."
Michael Jordan

"A strong positive self-image is the best possible preparation for success."
Dr. Joyce Brothers

"As one goes through life, one learns that
if you don't paddle your own canoe, you don't move."
Katharine Hepburn

"A BMW can't take you as far as a diploma or a degree."
Joyce A. Myers

**Success generally comes
from building on your strengths**

YOUR BEST CAREER

Throughout this book, you have been learning to identify your strengths (your interests, abilities and values) and match these to possible career choices. In the end, the career that best matches your strengths is likely the one that is going to bring you the greatest satisfaction. Having said this, it is also important to realize that other factors such as your level of education and/or training as well as the current job market will also have a strong impact on your career choice. Unfortunately some people may have a strong idea of which career is best for them but may be unable to get hired into this career because they lack the appropriate education/training and/or the job market is currently weak in this career area. As a result, it might be necessary to take a job that is not exactly what you were hoping for (although if you are really determined to be hired into the career that is best for you, then you should consider gaining the education or training necessary to be qualified for this career).

On page 68 is an activity which focuses on the concept of "related careers". In other words, if you can't get hired (for whatever reasons) into the career that you would love to do, perhaps there is a related "career" that might require less education and/or training and might even be in greater demand.

Page 69 provides a summary of your work in this book.

On page 68 is an activity

CHAPTER

4

"It is a funny thing about life: if you refuse to accept anything but the very best, you will very often get it."
William Somerset Maugham

> **"The indispensable first step to getting the things you want out of life is this: decide what you want."**
> Ben Stein (actor and author)

RELATED CAREERS

INSTRUCTIONS: It is possible that you might plan for a future career, but unforeseen circumstances (such as a changing job market, or not having the required education/training) might prevent you from successfully achieving this career. When this happens, it is beneficial to be aware that there are often many careers that are related to your main career choice. You might go in a slightly different direction while still choosing a career based on your interests, values and abilities. On the following chart, write one of your career choices (from page 64) in the circle in the middle of the chart. Next, write down all the careers that you can think of that are related. For example, if you wrote "doctor" in the middle circle some "related careers" might be nurse, medical supplies salesperson, x-ray technician, medical researcher, and so on.

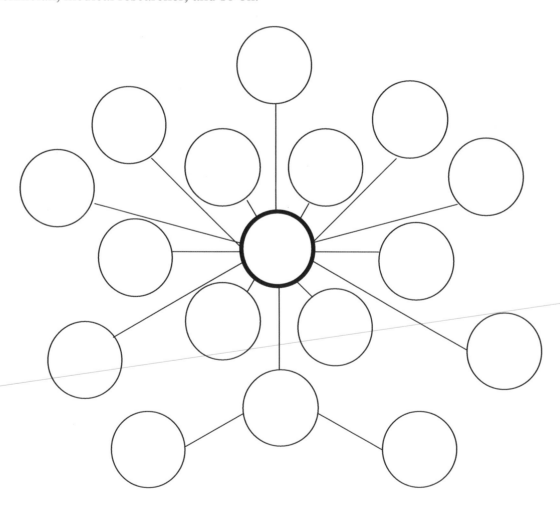

YOUR SUMMARY

INSTRUCTIONS: In BOX #1, write your top three interest areas from page 29. In BOX #2, write your top two abilities from page 54. In BOX #3, write your top three personal skills from page 54. In BOX #4, write your top 3 job specific skills from page 54. In BOX #5, write your top 3 values from page 63.

MY TOP 3 INTERESTS

1.
2.
3.

from page 29   **BOX 1**

MY TOP 2 ABILITIES

1.
2.

from page 54   **BOX 2**

MY TOP 3 PERSONAL SKILLS

1.
2.
3.

from page 54   **BOX 3**

MY TOP 3 JOB SPECIFIC SKILLS

1.
2.
3.

from page 54   **BOX 4**

MY TOP 3 VALUES

1.
2.
3.

from page 63   **BOX 5**

THE CAREER THAT IS BEST FOR YOU

Throughout this book you have identified careers that match your interests, abilities or strengths. Take another look at your career lists on pages 30, 55, and 64. In addition, take a look at your list of related careers on page 68.   From your career lists on these pages, select the three careers that you think would be best for you based on your strengths (see "your summary" on page 69), the current job market, and your level of education/training. Write these three careers in the box below.

THE CAREERS THAT ARE BEST FOR ME

1.

2.

3.

It is important to realize that there is often more than just one career that would be best for you. This is why you were asked to identify three careers in the above box.

Page 71 provides some thoughts on how to achieve your goals. These tips can help you begin your efforts to actually get hired into the career that is best for you.

The final chapter in this book provides some further thoughts on pursuing the career that is best for you.

TIPS ON ACHIEVING YOUR GOALS

1. Always write your goals down.
A goal not written down is not a goal.

2. Spend the greatest amount of your time each day on the things that
will have the greatest impact on you achieving your goals.

3. List all the ways both you and others will benefit
from you achieving your goals.

4. Keep a clear vision in your mind that shows you
having already successfully completed your goals.

5. Goals are best achieved when you break them into small,
sequential steps that have appropriate and definite timelines.

6. When you encounter an obstacle,
look for a new path that leads to your desired goal.

7. You can create your own good luck through hard work,
dedication to your goals, and believing you will be successful.

8. The biggest rewards in life are often when you move outside
your own comfort zone. Overcoming your fears
and taking risks often lead to the greatest successes.
Setting goals that will require a great deal of perseverance
often results in greater satisfaction
than quickly accomplishing easier goals.

9. The best way to kill an opportunity is to avoid taking it.
As you focus on your goals, always keep an open mind
for flexible ways of achieving them.

Most people struggle with success because of a lack of focus.

SOME FINAL THOUGHTS

Now that you have identified some possible careers that appear to be best for you, what do you do next? One of the most important aspects of becoming successful is related to your focus. It is critical to maintain your focus on what you really want. There may be times when it might be easier to compromise your values, interests and abilities and accept a career that is less than what you really desire. You can best prevent this from happening by forming a clear picture of what it is that you really want and keeping this picture in your mind at all times. Some people find it useful to actually find a picture representing the career they are looking for, or write the name of the career on a piece of paper. Keep this picture or the words constantly in your mind. It is important to clearly visualize yourself as being successful in pursuing this career. In addition, it may help you to keep a file of job advertisements or articles related to this career.

Once you believe that you can successfully get hired into this career, you will find a way to prove yourself right. We tend to get what we think about the most. When you think mostly about success, you will find success coming your way. When you think of the career that you want, clearly see yourself in the picture. When you are part of this picture, you will begin to move towards making it come true. Meaningful and lasting change starts first in our mind and then finds a way to become reality. Often, the key to becoming successful is changing what you are thinking about the most. Developing a positive attitude with a clear picture of what you want can be of tremendous value to you in achieving your dreams.

CHAPTER

5

"Whatever your mind can conceive and believe, you can achieve."
Napoleon Hill

Meaningful and lasting change starts first in our mind and then finds a way to become reality.

Now that you have identified your perfect career, you might find it useful to read my book *GET HIRED*. This book provides practical tips on marketing yourself, writing great resumes, finding the job you are looking for, writing effective cover letters, understanding how to best answer the questions that are most frequently asked in job interviews, and more. Information on this book is provided at the end of this book.

For those readers who are prevented from achieving the career of your dreams because of financial concerns, you might find my book *LIVE DEBT FREE* helpful to you. This book presents seven steps that you can apply to your life to gain financial security.

As has been stated at various times previously in this book, it is strongly recommended that you take your results from *CHOOSING YOUR CAREER* and discuss these with a qualified career coach, counselor or advisor.

What are you going to do with your life? I sincerely hope that you now have a few more answers.

> **"Destiny is not a matter of chance,
> but a matter of choice."
> William Jennings Bryant**

NOTES

GET HIRED

Brian Harris, B.A., M.Ed.

Learn six employer secrets that can improve your cover letter, resume, networking skills, and job interview results to help you gain employment in a new career.

Also by Brian Harris

Discipline Without Stress

Divorce and Children

Time Management

Live Your Dreams

How To Get A Job

College Success Tips

How To Choose Your College Major

Job Interview Tips

OTHER BOOKS BY BRIAN HARRIS

JOB SUCCESS
for high school students

175 Ready-To-Use Classroom Activities

Brian Harris, B.A. M.Ed.

MY FUTURE
Career/Educational Planning Activities For High School Students

150 Ready-To-Use Classroom Activities

Brian Harris, B.A. M.Ed.

THE STUDENT SUCCESS HANDBOOK
125 Ready-To-Use Activities

Includes activity handouts
and a 68 page student workbook

Brian Harris, B.A. M.Ed.

SELF-ESTEEM

150 Ready-to-use Activities to Enhance the Self-Esteem of Children
and Teenagers to Increase Student Success and Improve Behavior

Book 1

Brian Harris, B.A. M.Ed.

About the Author

Brian Harris is an award-winning teacher/counselor and best-selling author. He has extensive experience working in high schools, colleges, universities, and career counseling centers. He has achieved the designation of International Professional Speaker. Brian has a wide range of experience in the field of career/educational planning with both students and adults.

Brian lives in Burlington, Canada, with his wife and two teenaged daughters. In addition to writing, Brian is a part-time lecturer in counseling at Queen's University. He is also an accomplished artist (www.bcharris.com).

Brian enjoys family trips and is an avid canoeist and scuba diver.

Additional information about Brian can be found at

www.cgscommunications.com

59432988R00047

Made in the USA
Charleston, SC
03 August 2016